ANDRÉ HADLEY MARRIA

THE SONGS
I COULD NOT SING

A BOOK OF LIFE'S DESCRIPTIVE VERSES
WRITTEN ON THE PAGES OF A HEART—

COVER and AUTHOR PHOTOS: Teri Hurst-White, Dogwood Photography, Thomasville, GA.

All other photos: André Hadley Marria

Published by André Hadley Marria, Thomasville, GA

Online: www.SongsSpoken.com, www.AndreHMarria.com

A B O U T   T H I S   W O R K

I consider myself a serious spiritual mixture—a beautiful soul whose life has been lovingly, purposefully, and carefully documented on the canvas of time and a person who has always been a seeker of truth—my truth. It was easier to write my truths than to verbalize them. On my journey I hid in a wonderful haven of books and music, documenting my many thoughts, my wins, my losses, my hopes, and my dreams. Music became my constant companion. It has always been a major family theme. As a Hadley, it was understood that if you had a voice, you could and would sing as an expression of all your soul. In my own search for meaning as a child, I knew there was more to me than music, and therefore my voice was one that would not produce melodic chords. In being a seeker of my truth, I knew my inner voice would one day produce tones that spoke volumes about inner conflict, and if it were to speak at that time, the release would produce woeful sounds from my childhood and youthful stanzas of pain.

These pages began as an outpouring of perceptions and revelations of a child and her family history too troublesome to honor and too painful to forget. A beautiful black gifted family, not so different from any other gifted family that survived a troubled past, it was mine, and I was the middle child who often lived a life compromised for the peace of others.

The Songs I Could Not Sing is a collection of heart-gripping pictures and poems of love, friendships, beauty, and hope. It is a selection of words that reflect a spirit in search of acceptance and inclusion. They are thoughts that freed me from resentments and directed me in the pursuit of forgiveness. ***Many of us on this journey need to forgive our entire past transgressors and their transgressions.*** It is the healing of a heart, ***which begged for love, acceptance, and the coming of age.*** The discovery is that there was never a true separation. It's the celebration of an inner child achieving and acknowledging self-acceptance that she was a very significant part of the whole.

These pages contain thoughts, pictures, and stories of a life that has touched, shared, loved, and healed. It is an offering that embraces the belief that this act of sharing will lead others in the discovery of their true selves and to their own inner and outer rays of beauty and hope.

ABOUT THE ARTIST

André Hadley Marria is a Christian, wife, poet, therapist, mother, a woman for all seasons, and the author of a new book of life revealing poetry entitled "The Songs I Could Not Sing." A professionally trained singer and mental health counselor, Andre' shares short stories in a poetic style. She shares significant insightful episodes in her life that have created the verses of the "songs" she sings today.

André graduated from Fort Valley State College in 1973 with a B.S. degree in Music, and in 1975 with a degree in Mental Health Counseling. Her education and training have been ongoing, she considers herself to be a life-long learner and has used her skills for thirty-four years in service to the Georgia Department of Human Resources and many other organizations, clubs, and community groups. She is currently a Licensed Professional Counselor and a Certified Professional Counselor Supervisor.

Always seeking opportunities to mesh her two passions, the arts, and psychology, she organized a group called 3-D Whole Brain Productions wherein children were encouraged to exercise mental stretching through the arts. Practicing what she preaches, André has delighted audiences with her One- Woman Show performances.

Her community work is extensive. She is a Thomasville Entertainment Foundation Board of Trustee, Past Board Chair of Vashti Mental Health Center, a Trustee of Thomas County Chamber of Commerce, a past President of the Rotary Club of Thomasville, and a Distinguished Member of Toastmasters International.

The woman she has become is the result of family influence, being a wife of 47 years to Evangelist Walter Marria, Jr., mother to two birth children, two more given by God, as well as eight glorious grandchildren, and having had several exceptional experiences; most notably being a mental health first responder in the 9-11 Ground Zero Red Cross Disaster Relief Effort. They helped shape her perception of life and expanded her capacity for love and spirituality. It is authentically portrayed in this, her first published literary work.

WORDS AND PICTURES

"The Eye Is A Better Pupil"
to focus on the Beauty you will see.

My life is so incredibly connected to Nature on so many levels. As a child I remember spending hours looking at the stars, watching the waves in the water, looking at birds as they flew and animals as they crossed the distant creeks on roads into bushes.

I examined the way trees grew and how they would bend from one direction to the next; I then realized life has so much in correlation with nature. The clouds in the sky with movement going from west to east. The sun which rises slowly and sets so beautifully in the evening. The early morning biking, and late evening drives. My mind traveled to many places as I looked and took part in *the concert that I found in nature*.

More importantly, I found the healing of my soul; a healing that goes so deep within, and I continue to have this romantic relationship with nature.

The poems written, the pictures shared have always been a part of the professional work that I've done. I've used music, pictures and poems in my work as a therapist and have been amazed by the level of interaction with adults and youth in their ability to discover the hurt and pain in their own lives and the journey to healing.

The greatest joy is in being "in the moment" on the other side of all the uncertainty, struggles, and pain. It is all about being in the present... walking, talking, seeing clearly the "here and now"...one perfect whole note.

FORWARD

I am truly blessed for having traveled this road with my dear friend Dre, for more decades than we dare admit. Honored am I to have the opportunity to write this piece from within. Now, the world will know what I've known for a long time; that this sistah is about to challenge you, as a reader and as a writer, to reach deep within your mind and soul to bring forth your definitive, confident and determined vision. When I say "vision", I mean the power of your vision to propel your intellectual genius. Genius, she is, as a writer, as a person, as a visionary. This piece of work is not for the weak, unsteady nor blind. For you will find that her writings are from another place of tonetic peace. As I promised her, I will not fore-read, but knowing her as I do, I am confident that this work will leave you in tears, laughter, and bewilderment.

. As many of you may know, André is a talented vocalist, whose voice commands the trembling of all who hear her. Well, her writings are as powerful as her voice. Try to envision her words as musical dandelions dancing in a valley of love, forgiveness, and survival; now, embark upon this journey of no return.

J.Nell Ford — *Author*
Fort Valley State University Alumni

ACKNOWLEDGMENTS

These words are documented on the pages of my heart in memory of my mother and father, the late Ralphine Johnson Hadley and Morris B. Hadley, Sr. and my sister and brother, the late Theresa and Morris B. Hadley, Jr. Thanks also to my husband, Walter Marria, Jr., for his support and undying love. These individuals shaped and molded me through the lives they lived into the woman I am today.

I want to also dedicate this book to the memory of my grandmother, the late Rosetta James Hadley. This six-foot-tall, beautiful-inside-and-out black woman spoke volumes to me through her love, support, and wisdom, often spoken, often seen in the spirit.

Special thanks and recognition is extended to:

Debra Davison Bryant, my childhood friend whose eyes gave life to these pages ensuring the words truly reflected my deeper thoughts.

Teri Hurst White, "My Sister from another Mother," for capturing on this book cover, my favorite road often traveled as a child and more so NOW That I AM A Woman!!!

Rick Sherrell, my health coach and personal trainer, who knocked the dust off his publishing knowledge to help me expand this document into a book!

Last but none the less important...

J Nell Ford, My Fort Valley State College Soul Sister for fifty-one years. Our friendship began with our walks on that wonderful Fort Valley State College University Campus. She is a kindred spirit who saw me long before I saw myself... who shared in many of the formative struggles that included many happy and hungry days... who stuck closer than glue as we grew from dreamers to achievers! Thank you for the kind words regarding this book.

TABLE OF CONTENTS

1

SHARING THE STRUGGLES

THE STRUGGLE WAS REAL

Struggles come in many shapes and forms. They can be finding your way to the front door or finding your way through a storm. For me the struggle was...

...trying to figure out which way was the right way... which team was the winning team...

...which story was the true story... which adult was the stable adult...

...which way should I turn or what needs to be done. Everything was a struggle.

Do I walk in fear?

Should I discover God?

Who is God?

Why doesn't He care?

I was existing in a ball of confusion. What do I do now about my fear?

The struggle indeed was real.

So I sat in silence and wrote the stories that played over and over in my head. Fear, fear, fear!

During daybreak and early morn, during the lonely times, I would speak life to my silent friend. I would tell her to come to my place so that we could play, and just at the right time, I would say, "What are things like in your home? Does your brother get on your nerves?"

I am trying to figure out all the things that are going on in my home. Just when she was attuned, I would lose the courage to share my home.

When I think about home, it's easier to think about wide-open spaces, fields, and peace than to think of confusion, discord, and the lack of harmony. So as I escaped from the pain of reality, I would frame the pictures of life and how I wanted it to be!

WILL YOU COME HOME WITH ME?

Forgive me if I pause when I talk about home. It's my world, complex as it is, I'm proud of it. It isn't much, but it's home.

You see, Mama told me not to bring anybody home with me because somebody may see where she hides the whiskey she sold to feed me. And if that wasn't enough, she was ashamed of all the stuff we were busy hiding—the drinking, the fighting, the cutting, and stuff like that.

So when I ask you to come home with me, I am trusting that you understand that I have a lot of baggage that hasn't been put in the closet. I didn't know they were out. The closets are already filled with clothing that is dirty and stained.

Will you walk up the broken steps to my house? Watch out for the holes in the floor on the front porch. Come and see my room! Pay no attention to the cracks in the walls or the fact that you can see the sun through the roof and that it rains in every room of the house. We have no bathtub or hot water at bath time. Mama boils water for the tin tub, and I always bathe last.

You don't have to worry about feeling safe at night. They are long, lonely nights because Mama won't come home. You see we are often left alone on the weekends. That's when all of the drinking and fighting really gets out of control.

In the living room, we gather to fuss and cuss. Pay no attention to the anger you see on my face. I must look this way. It's safe. I don't take any mess. If you look at me a certain way, I'll get you! I don't get mad, I get even. It's the way of my home.

Come walk down the streets with me. Let's cross the road. The principal lives two blocks down the street, so I live in a good neighborhood. The teachers look down on me, though.

I won't guarantee you will meet my extended family. They are talented people. We sing and are educated. They are ashamed of how we live in my house, so everything is a secret. They don't want anybody to know just how messed up we really are.

We are learning to live a lie. One day I will change this! But not my sister. She turned to drugs.

Will you come home with me? It's pretty messed up, but it's home. My sister told me to tell you not to come. She said, "Don't bring your know-it-all attitude to our house." She said, "You have already judged me!"

Will you come...

Will you come... will you come home with me?

THERE COMES A TIME

There comes a time when an "evil wind blows no good," as the song says. You sense it, you feel it—that life as you know it will change. When it does, you blame yourself. Rarely do you think anyone else is the blame. You listen to the fights, you attempt to cover your ears, and then you just cry.

IS IT?

(1970–1972)

Silence through tears can give birth to conversations in the head and screaming in the heart. Is it so wrong for a child to not know how to face her fears?

Is it all right to smile on the outside with fears on the inside? Would it be too strange to hunger and thirst for empathy?

Is it better to keep secrets to preserve a name? Is it? Welcome to Hotel Pain!

Every child should feel protected, valued, and loved. Protected from harm, and the loss of innocence. In today's world, protection is hard to come by. It's a secret and very few will tell. The little one loses her way. Loses her voice, her pride, and her sense of self. She becomes a pawn, a useless kid. She learns to accept the lie, and then she dies.

PRISON

(APRIL 30, 1989, 1:05 P.M.)

When a child feels threatened in life... threatened by and fearful of the loss of family support and security. When a child has no understanding of normal or what should or should not be spoken she learns to become angry, withdrawn, a keeper of secrets. She becomes a stamp keeper, a clock watcher, a prisoner in her own mind.

Confusion around me,
pressured by the need to be heard,
so many stories to be told and so much blood to flow.
There is too much pain, too much blood, and no healing.
No time for tears,
no time for holding, and no time for healing.
No time for feeling that anyone really cares.

As I sit and hear, I have to plug up. I cannot hold back the tears. I wonder how many stories are being told.

Do people really want you to know?

What emotions do their songs in the key of life create?

Do I allow my heart of hearts to play my old tapes, or do I share the answers I have found?

Do I wait for another stage, another act, or exit stage left?

Impressive, original, and highly emotional.
Yet I see with my heart,
listen with my eyes and understand with my emotions.
So much knowledge, so much wasted time in yesterday. Oh! But it keeps
today intact!

The young–old, empty–full—Answers, anyone?

Where am I in all of this?

Bleeding, hurting, eyes around me searching for inner peace

—where am I, stepping into the next phase for me?

There are no real bottom lines here—

I stopped speaking for my language cannot be spoken—rebuild.

What do I see?

Beauty, pain, sadness, hope.

CONFRONTATION

Inner peace, baggy eyes, tired body, soul at rest.

Nakedness.

Pounding of one heart.

Spirits wandering in the night.

OOPS!

Words, feelings, and behaviors are difficult to separate sometimes, especially if they belong to you.

1. I've operated on levels of equality. OOPS!

2. I refused to timely equate devotion, loyalty, and trust with the necessary depth they deserved for proper development. OOPS!

3. The most dangerous: the human error we all make, but few admit — idolizing the existence of a few who possess qualities we all have, though they are hidden. OOPS!

TRUSTING

I must learn to let go and let God. I must accept myself with all my faults and that I am what I am because Ralphine was who she was. I must accept her choice of dignity and realize her anger was never at me.... but was at the disease. I must accept that my sense of security was lost, and I was afraid for many years after she died.

My achievements meant nothing because they were never validated by the person it was done for—my mom. Yet, as I validate it as a worthy accomplishment, I must make it mean something to me—for André.

Deserted early in life by my father for alcohol -- and later by my mother because of loneliness, emptiness, alcohol, and lastly, by death -- I felt if only I could have done something, then none of these things would have happened. How wrong I was.

As I learn to accept my life on life's terms, I am also learning to accept my anger, resentment, and emptiness. I am establishing within myself the ability to accept my father and forgive my mother for leaving and abandoning me. I am able to begin to understand me, the person I am today— one who feels she can go it alone when in essence I can't.

I need and trust you, God, to guide me.

OUR LAST LOOK

Silently, stilly it came. Death.

It entered the door to the room. It's partly dark

And as I cast my eyes towards the bed, there she was.

Resolved.

Protective of me and what she knew I could see.

A very small woman appearing three months pregnant.
There we were facing it. Death.

We both knew it.

BACK TO SCHOOL SHE SAID... and as I LEFT...
WE KNEW THIS WAS OUR LAST LOOK....

ARGUMENT

(7:25 A.M.)

He said, "They told me." She said, "Who is they?"

He said, "You should know." She said, "And so?"

He said, "They told me." She said, "And where?"
She said, "And I dare!"

He said, "They told me!"

She said, "It's a lie!" He said, "They told me."

She said, "You will die..."

He said, "They told me."

She said, "And destroy us?!"

He said, "They told me."

She said, "You don't love me!"

He said, "Enough."

She said, "Just go!"

He said, "And so?!"

She said, "I'll leave you!"

He said, "Just go."

He said, "They told me."

She said, "Destroying our love?"

He said, "They told me."

She said, "They are all lies."

"Pain never leaves us," she said.

"Others will destroy us," she said.

"Children will suffer," she said... and so.

WAITING

(MAY 6, 1977)

Waiting tears at my body and frightens my mind.

Fear causes my inner heart to retreat and desert the idea of facing reality.

Admitting it is the answer.

Waiting makes me feel I am not good enough. Waiting is an art.

It causes many vibes to pour forth,

And harness all the energy that makes one brave.

Yet sometimes the coward is caught up in the waiting process.
Waiting is in eternity...

HE WAS MY NIGHT WATCHMAN

Growing up, everyone knows you are daddy's girl, or at least that is what you think and feel. Every opportunity you get to spend time in his shop, fishing, or eating is an awesome affair. Then one day you realize it was all because of another mission that you had no part to play.

You can call him Daddy. I thought of him as my playmate and friend. Our fun would begin at 3:00 a.m. when he would return from his adventures. He would get me up, and we would eat breakfast. He would cook eggs and toast, and as I rubbed the sleep from my eyes, he would fry the bacon. Mama and Jr. slept gently through the night while we ate and drank milk. Then it was back to bed again. He was my night watchman.

A watchman has the duty to warn, protect, and defend. Isn't that right, Daddy?

THE BATON

(JANUARY 21, 2003, 11:30 A.M.)

If I take it

Will you still be there?

Will you stand with me and help me when my spirit has grown weary?

 It is such a troubled world

So much to be done

I'm seeing so much as I grow

If I take this baton and begin this work,
will I do well with that which must be done?

Oh, I doubt myself, my ways, my will,

I've wearied much since you've been gone.

Yet your spirit is here

Oh yes, I feel you near

It is the face my soul longs to see

So, I close my eyes and the tears come through.
If I cry long enough, will I be able to see you?

Oh, this baton you have given me is hard to handle and hold on to.

You held it right. It seemed so right.

I knew it would belong only to you....

but you passed it on!

So, I know you are gone.

But how I long to see your face

As I take this thing that is attached to the dream....

Please stay near sweet P.

I need you when I take it.

Will I see you?

Will you stay?

Oh, I hear you.

You will always be there!

AT NIGHT AS I SLEPT

(NOVEMBER 9, 2002, 7:30 P.M.)

At night, I believe one Saturday night, while I slept in my mother's bed my uncle slipped in while I slept and began to play his games.

I knew not what to think or feel.

It hurt at first... and then he said, "If you tell, I'll make your life a living hell."

I grew to hate myself at first, my mother as well.

She must have known what he had done and failed to protect me from this hell.

The shadow hangs over me when men come close. I trust no one who says they love me.

My family loved me, so they said, and it was a sting of eternal pain.

Who am I now? What have I become?

It's not easy to be seen.

The makeup covers all the stains!

Healing is slow, they say,

In time, I began to see change. My yesterdays of blue are gone.

And I released the guilt I felt and my uncle's name.

I've grown to be a woman now, and though the pain is gone my life is different from then.

I've learned to change life's tone,

I know what it takes to overcome. I know the importance of trust.

I can say my tears were a healing. It was never my fault he thirsted.

2

CONVERSATIONS WITH MYSELF

HOW DO YOU RECONCILE?

How do you reconcile a deep emotional deformity developed due to abandonment?

Abandoned by your mom, your dad.

Rejection. Emptiness

Never feeling loved. Anger

Needing to be needed. Resentment.

Pride. Determination.

Leadership through anger and pride

Anger the major motivator to success

Rejection

Loneliness

Insecure.

You gave, but never received or never felt like you received

How do you reconcile?

Sleepless nights?

Fears?

RESENTFUL

(FEBRUARY 8, 2017, 2:40 P.M.)

I'm resentful of my mother dying and leaving so many unanswered questions
 which have caused so much pain in my ability to accept life on life's terms.

The cause: I was left alone and afraid

Affects my ability to trust anyone. My sense of security.

I am resentful of my father who gave me nothing to hold on to

For choosing to give to others rather than to his own children

For failing to care for me during the darkest hours.

The cause: his lack of self-worth and alcoholism

Affected by tolerance of others with no commitment or sense of purpose affects
my sense of security.

I am resentful of my brother

The cause: his selfishness and superior attitude

Affected my self-esteem

I was always known as Morris Hadley's little sister

André was not known

I am resentful of myself for the need to control

The cause: unrealistic expectations, pressure to perform, trying to be all things to all people.

Affects my mental health, stability, inner peace, and self-love

I am resentful of myself in my home life

The cause: my inability to keep it calm and give quality time and love

Affects my self-esteem, my security

I am resentful of my extended family for being so messed up

The cause: false sense of importance

Affected my personal relations with my family.

Affected my pride

ANSWERS, ANYONE?

(MARCH 24, 1977, 3:02 P.M.)

Volcano of vibes electrified by a touch of tenderness. Emotions within.

Thorns in the flesh. Tears. Baby's first cry. The cheers.

Happiness. The vapors. Unknown sadness. The noticeable... never gone.

Emotions within.

Eyes shining with age.

Wrinkles of youth with power to save.

Reaching out but hurting within. Emotions all killing!

Drugs, clicks... future shock

6:30 p.m. news

Hands stretched across the land.

Answers, anyone?

WHERE IS GOD?

It was He that I needed! Him to hear me! I lost my voice, my faith, and my ever-after when you left! Now where is God?!

ONE-EIGHTH NOTE

I witnessed your dance of relief, for you had no solace,

And all I had of reality was you Mama.

What was a little girl to do? I listened to your pain.

He spoke of your loneliness as he sang his song.

BEAUTY FOR ASHES

For every picture in my mind that I have of pain and heartbreak, I have pictures of beauty and God's grace!
I could always find joy in nature. Many times, I just sat still looking at God's universe and feeling assured

he had better things for me to do...

better things.

I would rise early in the mornings to kiss the morning sun

What joy I would feel before dealing with the hand that was dealt me each day.

LOOKING AT ME

(FEBRUARY 5, 1989, 11:40–2:30 A.M.)

Looking at my own mistakes... where have I been selfish?

In relationships and selfishly seeking my own personal goal and not allowing myself to receive. I promised God I would never treat anyone as I had been treated. Therefore, I give all I have and cripple people to a point of dependency. That is my biggest sin. I have been self-seeking in the name of helping others. I just don't understand why.

People I have hurt by my conduct: My love—not sharing the real me

My sister—not being honest with the fact that I never really liked her ways. attitude

I am willing to straighten out the past. I can't with my sister—the person I see is too sick to hear the truth from me.

IT'S A SANDBOX AFFAIR

(JANUARY 30, 2013, 9:50 P.M.)

To share or not to share.

The conflict of my inner child.

The mental playground of my soul.

It's a sandbox affair.

To be honest in my core,

to pretend that I want to share,

or should I just shovel?

I really don't care

so I honor the conflict of my inner child as I journey through the pages of my life.

It is all about sharing, growing, and giving among all the messages we receive in life.

It's a sandbox affair I have with my inner child - the playground of my inner soul.

It's my affair with my life that I must honor, trust, and behold.

AIN'T IT FUNNY?

(FEBRUARY 10, 1981)

Sometimes it's heartbreaking to stop briefly, looking back from whence you came, but it's necessary if I am to keep a perspective as to where I am going.

My eyes filled with tears as I rode through the streets where I played. It's as if time had taken me back to yesterday. I could hear the ole gang playing in the streets, and Mama calling me in for the evening. Oh, how I hated nights!

There was Chico, Tim, Jabo, Pistol Pete, Little Junior, Bubba, Little Scott, Baby Brother - and then there was me. We played by the streetlights and starlight...

But those are only memories today. The streets are paved, the houses old, and the people have moved or gone by way of death. I guess I spent thirty minutes driving and looking, remembering how carefree and young I was.

Of course, the tears came, and as usual, I would not let them fall. My selfishness will be the death of me!

As I returned home, my own house was filled with the noise of my own children, asking some of the same questions I probably asked my mama... "Where have you been, Mama?"

Funny how times just slips right on away!

I WANTED TO SAY SOMETHING

(AUGUST 22, 2001, 10:00 P.M.)

I wanted to say something to you tonight and the line was busy so I would not call back.

I wanted to say something to you and words got in my way.

I wanted to say something to you tonight and my heart was beating too fast.

I wanted to say something to you tonight and I realized that years separate us in thinking.

I wanted to say something to you tonight but time was moving too quickly.

I wanted to say something to you tonight but you would not hear me, so I sat and looked at this damn computer and said something to myself.

You are much more than this, I said. Fear is not an option.

You're much more than this and tomorrow is not promised, so here is what I did.

I write these words that only I could really see and feel and what a rush and release I experienced.

3

VERSE 3

LOVE AND FRIENDSHIP

THE MAN I LOVE IS YOU

Loving someone is easy when you see the inner beauty they possess.

I see you.

I see the beauty in your smile

and the wonderful way you ask "What's going on?"

I see you as you lay next to me and curl

as only you can and then put your favorite fingers near your face

as an assurance and sign that there is still that little child within.

Loving you is easy.

You have the loving yet firm arms of support

that are always there for me during my lonely hours.

You never invade my private space.

You are the man I love.

I see the beauty of your walk

as I watch you from afar,

the beauty of your arms

as they swing in the music of your walk,

the downward gaze and upward look in the motion of your stroll.

You are my hero, my bright and shining star.

I see you!

When you bend to gently kiss me before leaving in the morning,

I feel You.

I feel the color of your love.

The kiss again upon your return at the end of your day.

I see your beauty.

If I could briefly share a few thoughts of you

they would be...

You are the butter in my jam,

the joy in my song,

the gift I requested of God.

I am thankful for the love that you give.

The man that I love is you!

In closing this never-ending story,

I cherish most your love.

The faith you have in our heavenly father.

The commitment you have made to Christ

the values you instilled in our children,

The example you live with me.

When I awake each morning

you are there.

When I fall asleep at night

you are there.

In the middle of the night when I am fast asleep

you reach for no reason, to kiss me as you turn.

I feel the beauty and color of your love.

You are the man that I love,

and I am so very blessed to call you my friend.

Loving you always

André the wife of 26 yrs.

—*December 6, 1999*

TEACHER

(APRIL 10, 2001)

A small room shared by two on Stevens Street.

Youth and experience—

the student and the teacher.

Book, music, and the two—

A wonderful experience shared by me and you.

Lessons in life. Travels through time.

The sharing of things. A gift of a dog. Lessons in leaving.

Uniting in time.

The passage of time has served us well.

We've built a bond tied by the hands of God.

We have shared our laughter and our tears.

Thank you for holding my hands when others saw them not.

For teaching me about the real world—

about just being me...

doing what I wanted to do.

For loving me unconditionally.

For sharing your life,

your world with me.

I want to just thank you for making me a valuable part of your life.

For piercing my ears...

I'm still smiling about that.

Nancy Wilson

Kahlil Gibran

Nancy Wilson

My first trip to Atlanta

The Gingerbread House

Me as Mahalia Jackson

my first competition outside of Thomasville

Loving me enough to fight for our friendship

Nancy Wilson

Dinners. Smiles, Rejections, Acceptance.

For giving me you and all the tomorrows, we have to share.

All that I ask is that you allow me to share all your tomorrow's journeys

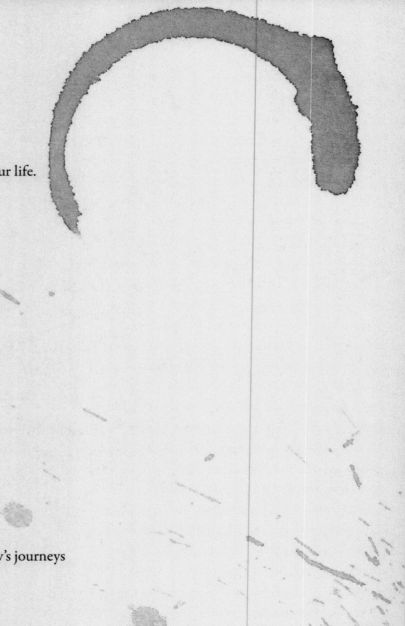

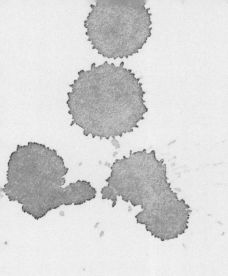

That I be at your side for any roads crossing and bumps along the way.

For any new discoveries, for we have done our walks together.

Allow me to be the wind beneath your wings.

For any strength I have to stand or walk has you at its foundation.

I see the beauty of life through your eyes.

For many days I would not have seen had it not been you

For you are the Diva Teacher

I am happy to have you in my life

You are a part of my soul

"For you are loved with a love that is greater than love"

 whose foundation was given and shaped by you in love

Always and forever

—*André Hadley Marria*

MAMA PALMS

(DECEMBER 27, 2017, 7:52 P.M.)

Small in stature.

White hair with a radiant face, strong will, strong spirit.

Asking, never answering questions.

My eyes were opened to see God's hand.

Mama Palms was my mentor, major professor, and second mom.

Many nights sorting through my stories. Helping me to see my own strength and light.

A storyteller. A song.

A condition. A legacy.

Strength through my storm. Tooled me to rewrite my story.

Helped me walk hand in hand with my strong black man.

Pushed me to use my wings.

Daily I celebrate her story and her song.

IF YOU KNEW ME

(*for Jimmie Nell*, APRIL 23, 2000, 6:40 P.M.)

If you knew me, would it matter that I'm not real?

Or would my appearance fool you -
my dress and physical appeal?

My stature is not striking, my laughter loud and true,

But if I share my darkest thoughts,
would you believe they are true?

I have a heavy load to carry, burns which stain the soul.

If you really knew me, would you really let me belong?

I have a burning desire to show you all my terrible scars.

If you saw them, would you believe I got them
by battling other gods?

If you really knew me, would you really believe?

I need you to be with me, as I allow myself to bleed.

I've taken off my mask. My stature is weak and frail.

I need you to hold and see me before I reach my grave.

If you really knew me, would you think my smile was real?

Or can I still fool you, continuing to act as though
I'm real?

I want to stop pretending.

I need a place I can ask you to accept me by reaching,
talking to me, accepting me.

Naked before you I stand!

REAL LOVE

I took your hand.

You walked in.

You saw

I felt.

YOU GAVE.

I AM HERE

You are gone.

I waited.

You returned.

IF

(MAY 2, 2000, 12:18 A.M.)

If I take your hand and walk with you into the doorway of freedom

do you promise to honor the gift?

If I told you this was just the beginning of your ability to:

see

sense

feel and just be

would you honor your strength?

passion and desire

then believe in yourself.

If I told you that you already know how to fly

would you spread your wings and take flight?

YOU, YOUR EYES, YOUR SMILE

(MAY 2, 2000, 12:21 A.M.)

Your expressions

Your shyness

Your anticipation

Your acceptance

Your desire to explore

Your desire to just be

Your acceptance of your strength

is love to the nth degree

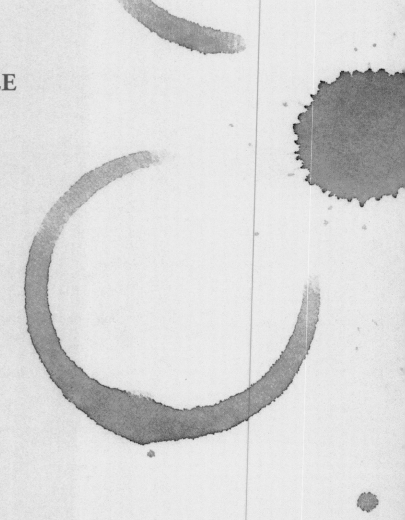

YOU AND ME

(DECEMBER 5, 1976, 9:00 A.M.)

You have been good for me

Reaching into the back of my mind and touching my soul

You say all the things I love to hear

And you paint the pictures of the life I need to see.

in the gallery of my mind.

Outside I am cold

Yet you know what I need

and you give that to me

You are gentle, yet warm

Wanting so little, giving so much

Yet when you reach out for my hand

I am cold....

you hit a wall

It's the one I created to protect me

When I reach again

I know I will touch and feel your love

You are forever with me

Your forces are powerful

yet calm...

you allow so much...

you accept so much from me.

I take from you only the parts

of that which I would like to be

You are my oasis in the desert

I could eat of your pain

Love and understanding

Yet you would never miss it

This I know you would do for me

One day, I will be able to just be

Not mentally, but spiritually

To many I am, to you, I could be

That is why you are so important to me

I have learned from you

that if I expect nothing

I will receive everything

The past

Present

and future constitute reality

and with you, I can live that reality

because the forces demand it...

they demand that I give...

and I need to give

All I can give...

because of you!

ETERNITY IS

The space we share in the unknown

The infinite range of emotions

Spoken without words

the stroke of affection received in each spoken word

Changing of forms, patterns, and spirits

Time shared by me

A sensitive lover with blood of fire

waiting to pour out on those who pass by

Passing is never done in eternity

only experienced by you and me

Eternity is an infinite

sensitive lover

controlled by timeless passionate space

Eternity is.......

YOU ARE

You are here...

I feel you

You never left

It's my fear...

my lack of faith.

It's your hands over mine

which guide me now that you have gone

Shining eyes that light my morning sky

I see you

CHOCOLATE

"Written for Double Touch Chocolate" Dr. W. Mary Price Langley

MAY 3, 2000, 7:30 PM

You were:
Bearing the Burden
Feeling the Pain
Living the fear
Embracing your Faith

You Achieved it!!
You were:
Raising your Granddaughter
Without your son
Traveling the State of Georgia
Working your Magic

Helping others
You were:
Burning more than the midnight oil
You were learning the "truth"
About your "Spiritual Roots"
Black Men in the Pulpit

You Were:
Learning you had Cancer
You were learning to live with Cancer
You are Surviving Cancer!!!!
You were Tireless and Determined
You Made it!!!

You were being a friend standing with me as my father slipped from life to death
You were taking care of your mother
You were talking about being a nanny, the taxi, Kelly girl and
Releasing the stress when talking to "Sweet Chocolate" .... That is me!

Who would have thought it????
I knew, if anyone could overcome these challenges, it would be you!!!
You Are:
A Woman of Consistency
You Are a Woman of Determination
You are a Woman of Great Faith
You are a Woman of Humor
You are a Woman of Purpose
You Are
My Friend
—*André H. Marria*

WHERE I HIDE MY THINGS

There is a place I go where no others can find

A place where I can hide my things as well as hear my mind

I think a lot about things

No other asked what I thought

I can let my feelings out and say the things I feel

There is no one there to tell me NO!

I'm safe and I am real

It's my home away from home...

a place that I can build

I can put my anger there!

I can hate my sister there!

I can hate my mother there!

I can learn how to figure out why I feel as I do there.

There is no judgment there

It's my place that's real

I am tired of being left alone

so I go to my place where I can hide my things

and be left totally alone......

IF EVER

(JUNE 17, 1977)

If ever I have sought an answer to my existence, God has given my quest the end it so rightly deserves.

If my heart has ever needed to give love, God has given the increase.

If ever my soul has searched for union with its soul, God has made you.

If ever my conscience needed unity, God has given the power to help my spirit find contentment.

If ever yesterday left doubt in love, today God has revealed all I must experience in you.

And now I wake with new security, accepting what I know is so rightly mine.

Now I can lose all chains on old feelings -- feelings that once appeared too dangerous, much too damaging.

Now I can regress to a supplicating, dependent little child. For we are all children, adults, and children again.

If I ever needed reassurance that:

... the floor is stable,

... love is without limits,

... people can be sincere,

... you love me,

... you give out of knowing I need and deserve,

I have found my life, myself more than worthy to live!

GRACIOUS DESIGN

(DECEMBER 24, 2017, 11:00 A.M.)

Impeccable in movement.

Smooth and purposeful in your stride.

Beauty inside your often-felt pain.

You, my love, you are a gracious design.

Spirited in your speech.

Resourceful under pressure.

My rock, my shelter on this journey of mine.

You, my love, are a precious design.

Hopeful when I'm distressed.

Strong, nevertheless.

My water. My joy. My peace of mind. You, my love, are my strength.

My lifetime hopeful, beautiful, precious, gracious design.

MY PERFECT JOY

(*An Ode to Zion*, FEBRUARY 6, 2013, 9:30 A.M.)

2001 was a year of losses. There was 9/11.

There was me working as a first respondent.

Seeing the bodies come up from the pit, as it was known.

Listening to the firefighters speak as if it was just a job to protect their vulnerability.

The loss of my second grandson to my only daughter.

Time is the answer.

His time,

not ours

We just have to wait

One night in a large bright place you came in full array

Red, fighting and yelling your battle cry!

You were not concerned about others' concern

Your head tilted to your right, you declared, I am here!

You had no knowledge of our fears

our past losses

our past pain and tears.

You were only concerned with now!

So you fought

They said neonatal care

You said get it done

I am here!

and so, I smiled to think

God granted me the perfect gift

at the right time

in the right place

He allowed me to see my firstborn

my only daughter,

now a woman, bring forth her blessing

Dee Dee said you were her second chance.

She named you Zion Mariah Williams

I call you My Perfect Joy.

THE CANVAS OF TIME

DEAREST AUNT LULA, JANUARY 3, 2015

There are many Memories hidden in the heart of a child. They nourish the spirit and give birth to joy in the little things. You have left those kinds of memories in my heart as a child and I am sure you never knew it. I vividly remember your visits home when you lived in New York and how often you, Uncle George, mom and dad enjoyed your times together.

It was on one of those visits that we were at Mother's house, and you tucked me in bed one evening. You said, "Children need to get their rest, and should be fast asleep by 8:00 PM. Get your rest and we will see you in the morning." You kissed me good night and then you were off for the evening with Uncle George, mom, and dad. It's amazing how I believed that and went fast asleep! To others here tonight this may not mean a thing, but to me, it was everything as a child.

Tonight as you celebrate your 80th birthday, I salute you for having time for children.

A pearl is highly regarded for its beauty or value. Thank you for leaving pearls. The value of your pearl brought joy and happiness to a child. It was given as *"**Time and Attention; a Touch and a Smile**."* There are many memories hidden in the heart of a child. They nourish the spirit and give birth to joy in the little things. Thank you for leaving pearls on my "canvas of time."

Happy 80th Birthday!

Love Your Niece,
André Hadley Marria

THE BEAUTY OF EVERYTHING WAS IN HER EYES

(A TRIBUTE TO MY AUNT ESTELLA HADLEY GROOVER, MARCH 1, 2015)

Dearest Aunt Estella,

As I write this tribute in deep appreciation of your love, I want you to know that I sincerely thank you for being a wonderful, gentle, kind, and loving soul. May God continue to bless you with many more years to write and share your love! Below is my tribute to you:

The eyes communicate love in many ways. For me, it was through your eyes, Aunt Estella.

It was through your hands which you carefully made dresses here and alterations there placing your designs which were your signature for good work! When you were pleased, ***the beauty of everything was seen in your smiling eyes***! Oh how they sparkled when you were happy, and that was all the time.

Words are used to ask for things, but it was Aunt Estella's eyes that somehow knew what I wanted and there it appeared! Her Pepsi! As she sat on the front porch with Mother and I sat on the steps laughing I would say, "I caught you. Can I have some?" The laugher of her voice could reach the sky!

To me Aunt Estella, you were tall in stature and a master artist in the Kitchen. The Sweet aroma in your house was the result of tenderness. I would taste the cake and see the pleasing smile in your eyes knowing that I really loved it. ***The Beauty of everything was in your eyes!***

There was not a day that you did not visit with Mother. I was there at every visit and those precious times were spent sitting on the front porch laughing and talking, watching our favorite day time television shows before daddy came home from work. You set the wonderful example of how a child should honor your parents, having a meaningful relationship, loving them, trusting them and learning to share life's up and downs with them. Thank You for such a precious lesson! You are and were a teacher, a sermon I could see. You walked the walk!

You are a woman of few words. On honors night, my senior year in high school, unknown by me, my name was called to receive a scholarship from the Eastern Star! You never mentioned at any time you were doing this. You never spoke of it once, and to this day it has not been a big deal with you. It meant everything to me! If it were not for you, I would not have gotten that! Thank You!!! ***The beauty of everything that I see and have always seen comes from your loving Eyes! They shine so bright Aunt Estella! Keep Smiling, Keep shining! You are Beauty and you are loved.***

Your Oldest Niece,
André Hadley Marria

OVERCOMING WITH HOPE

UGLINESS

(JANUARY 4, 2018, 6:06 P.M.)

Been trying to understand

why it is necessary to hold a person down

There are all kinds of ugliness in this ole world

Seen people plot to save their kind

Take my talents of any kind

Change my truth to speak their lies

There are all kinds of ugliness in this town

Standing on my own, I stood alone

Couldn't count two souls to stand with me

Not many honest

bold or strong

Ugliness knows no color

has no character, I am told

Ugliness is a tale

professionals rarely discuss or admit exists

Won't condemn!

Can't be eradicated!

It has a place in our society

to serve the privilege

shameful, oh, so wrong!

I won't wear it!

declare it!

bow down to it!

I won't respect it!

or share it!

Ugliness will never take a place

or have a place in my heart and soul.

TEACHER IN SILENCE

I learned a lot from my daddy in silence. I learned to pay attention to details.

My daddy painted cars in the shop he owned. He said very little, but he looked intensely at every dent, every mark, and every indentation. He carefully taped every seam and every line to cover what was not to be harmed.

I learned that 'half-efforts' were not enough. What you perfect is your signature. I saw this as he would step back and look for anything that was not in perfect alignment.

I learned the importance of sticking with it, not deserting the effort, the importance of following through, knowing that everything you do is your signature.

I learned from my daddy the importance of loving what you do and the satisfaction that comes with knowing that you made a difference in the quality of work that you performed. Then I learned to leave it alone when the job is done.

The importance of silence when you are doing something—demands you concentrate and be focused. Even though I was sitting there with him, he never chided me or made me feel that I was in the way. The only thing he demanded of me was my silence. He did not see me. There was a lot of work ethics taught in that! I missed it then. I see it now! Daddy was a great teacher in silence.

WHAT I LEARNED FROM MY MAMA

There are many things in life I have learned:

I learned from my mama the importance of having your own business and learning to have your own. She had her own beauty shop. It was the local place where all the ladies would gather, especially on Tuesdays to get their hair done.

I learned from Mama the art of conversation. Man! She could converse. And not only that, she was also an investigator, always clarifying fiction from fact! In today's world, we might call that gossiping, but then, through the eyes of a child, she searched for the facts!

To them it was a community affair to discuss what child was not being reared right, what a mother should have done differently "to keep that child out of jail." And me, of course, I sat and listened, feeling important. I was chosen to be an integral part of such an event, to hear all the stories they shared. Of course, when the most important issues were being discussed, I was always asked to exit the shop.

As I reflect, I loved the smell of the hair burning, the curling irons heating, refilling the kerosene burner, and the fellowship and power a group of women who supported each other possessed. What joy they had and the happiness and laughter they shared!

I learned from Mama the sense of caring for the community. If you needed sugar, we sent a cup. She taught us to give even out of our lack.

I guess I learned from my mama the importance of relationships. It is always important to have people around you who care.

EVER-CHANGING

Looking through the window, there is much to see.

Troubles of many kinds

visions we rarely allow ourselves to see.

What is best of all the views is the picture of truth you are forced to see.

It can free you,

destroy you

strengthen you

or serve you to be all you can be.

It's a temporary window confronting the stories that can set you free.

You are never defined by circumstances.

You learn to understand them.

You accept that who and what you are changes...

to be bold, to be black, and to be beautiful.

Solid as a rock.

Bright as a star!

Ever-changing!

Ever-changing! Ever-changing!

When we look closely to the hills

and see the skies and the trees,

we can't help but find hope.

In the midst of fear,

I am always encouraged by the presence of the Holy One.

As I grew and learned,

I came to know Him.

In the midst of my struggles, I

came to trust Him.

Escaping, I would ride through the woods,

and as I would ride,

I always found peace around me.

Knowing Him

and growing in Him

gives me peace and acceptance

I am bold, black, and beautiful!

Solid as a rock!

Bright as a star!

Ever-changing! Ever-changing! Ever-changing!

BEGINNING NEW BEGINNINGS AGAIN

As I start toward new beginnings, I take with me new patience, new hope, new courage and a deeper understanding of who I am. The end of old programs and reruns, station breaks, and current events on some poor soul who knows not his beginning and has little knowledge of the human touch and where he is to end.

New Beginnings Again?

...trying to find feelings again.....trying to love again

...trying to give respect again

...knowing this beginning has yet another end.

Beginning new again... only toward newer beginnings again can this soul become one with self and this same self's friend.

DREAM BUILDERS

Dream builders are those of us who begin to develop in all sorts of places.

We reach for difficult heights.

We achieve the impossible early on in our journey.

In this very room you have reached the place where peaceful waters flow.

Exceptional minds are constantly in motion.

Respect the mess. Appreciate the energy!

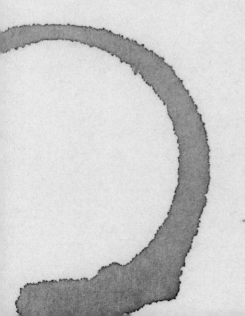

I'M STILL HERE!

There must be work for me to do, I'm still here.

There must be work for me to do, I'm s-t-i-l-l here.

Broken, wounded, and bitter from deceitfulness.

Troubled and tired and no vision of relief!

I'm still here!

Broken and bewildered, shaken with disbelief!

Upward I look... a place of refuge.

I seek focus and redirection.

Upward I stand, not defeated, a real woman. I'm still here... I'm still here...
I'm still here!

ENOUGH IS ENOUGH

(MARCH 3, 2004, 11:12 A.M.)

There are gaps in the spaces of our lives where we need to mend.

Gaps which represent a tearing away, separating, or parting from relationships, friendships, and even our souls

Even so, there is also a need for healing, coming together of sorts.

A filling in. Even the mending of our hearts, minds, and souls.

Building bridges over troubled friendships, relationships,

even our hearts and souls must be an inner work—

One that is carefully and purposefully done with beams of hope, not beams of steel. Pillars of love, not pillars of stone.

Walls of trust not walls of concrete. Covers of honesty, not wire-held beams.

When enough is enough, go within!

Nurture your spirit by facing the truth about yourself and your needs.

Become one with your identified purpose.

Unfold the love you must have for you and believe that you are worthy to be loved.

Take an honest inventory of your life this very moment.

Trust that in God's universe, nothing happens by chance.

You are where you are for a reason.

Sit with the experience, learn the lesson, flow in your spirit.

Build bridges of love, hope, and honesty, and trust in each step you take.

Realizing enough is enough!

IRON THAT SHARPENED IRON

(JULY 21, 2001, 2:55 P.M., *written by André Laretta Hadley Marria for the Atkinson, James, and Related Families Reunion*, JULY 20–22, 2001)

We should consider ourselves a serious spiritual mixture; beautiful souls whose lives have been lovingly, purposefully, and carefully documented on the canvas of time—people who must be seekers of our truth.

How do we determine depth? The intensity of strength?

The fathom of the ocean? The measure of a man?

...we don't, we simply guess.

Our forefathers, our ancestors have been our strength and we were their hope. How have we measured up? For they were the roots.

And we represent branches from their tree. From whence come our strength, our drive, our ambition?

Our ancestors, grandparents, and parents.

What debt do we owe?

A better world we must build.

A clearer vision, we must see!

What we have become is the result of the roots from our family tree

Our mothers' love, our fathers' strength, our sisters' love, our brothers' endurance are all because of this family tree. What legacy do we leave?

They were sturdy, strong, seasoned, yet mighty in deeds. This and all of this is the result of our family tree.

As we gather to remember, to savor the taste of their labors of their love, we must never lose sight of their beautiful light and their untiring, long, hard, and burdensome labors of work and love.

Always dependable! Always there!

Their feet and hands, both made of clay, but truly iron that has sharpened us.

Separate, yet equal as we live miles apart.

But in heart, we are iron, we are clay.

We are the iron -- our ancestors have sharpened us with their hearts.

5

VERSE 5

MY EARTH SPEAKS

NATURE

(DECEMBER 27, 2017, 3:30 P.M.)

The universe has always been my close companion. As a child I stargazed. It was as if heaven opened its window every evening and gave me a heavenly show. A concert. I would lie in the grass with my knees tucked and sing songs which brought joy to my soul! What a lovely way to spend weekend evenings!

Riding through the woods brought similar joy. Smelling that red Georgia clay and watching the sun through the early morning breeze. I would stop along the way and pick up rocks. Wondering what story was in each crevice.

On weekends my parents would go fishing in Florida, and Daddy would buy us yellow t-shirts, blue pants, red buckets with shovels. As he and his friends would go out on the boat, Mama and her friends would watch us as we played along the shore! These were some of the happiest moments I can remember!

Seashells were my favorite water souvenirs. My brother and I would run ahead of each other competing on who would find the biggest shell. These times near the water began a lifelong love of the sea. Today, during the winter of my years, I find immense joy walking, listening, sitting, cuddling near the sea!

PEACE

Walking through the woods with my lifelong companion brings joy!

I see God in each sound of the birds as we walk the canyon floor. I feel His presence when I see the rainbow through the trees.

Each step is taken as a child beginning a new day of discovery! What a day, walking through the concert in the woods.

Sitting at the edge of time, looking out on His wonder! Such contentment! Trees bending with time, saying step through and I will salute you!

One look cast upon the mountains, and you cannot help but feel one with the universe. Such inner peace!

Red flowers under a sometimes-cloudless sky, I can't help but wonder what it must have been like before so many of us populated this world. Canopies that are heavenly divine. Waterfalls pouring out of rocks speaking volumes in sounds! Peaceful music to my soul.

What a lovely time to be alive!

HEAVENLY SUNLIGHT

Heavenly sunlight!

Morning mist.

Clouds looming over the ocean waves.

Such a healing, such a relief.

Happiness without, rejoicing within.

Heavenly sunlight with the breeze ringing in my ears.

CONTENTMENT IN THE WATERS

When I sit and listen to running water, it is then I feel contentment.

When we find contentment within our souls, we have found the Lord and know the joy of the Lord.

Be never separate nor apart from a diligent search of His Word.

He is the Healer and Ruler of this vast universe. When we understand the true meaning of free-flowing waters, it can be a cleansing to our souls. He certainly has been for me.

I sat for hours looking and listening, and with each ripple made, there was a renewed sense of healing that nothing is impossible with God. If He is my stabilizing anchor, then I too can help others find their anchor!

Have you ever had water speak to you? Sit and listen sometimes, and I promise you, if there is ever trouble inward, you just may feel renewed! It can certainly be a place to feel safe!

GRATITUDE

Thank you for the vision to see green trees, blue skies, and your birds. Thank you for letting me feel your presence. Thank you for letting me look beyond faults of my own and express my needs.

I am grateful for this present time. This new opportunity to begin again.

Thank you for allowing me to hear an old phrase stated differently: love is what it does.

Thank you for letting me come face to face with the challenge of a new person in whom lies answers and who hopes for self and others.

Thank you for time, tolerance, and patience.

KISSING THE SUN

(CALIFORNIA, JANUARY 7, 2018, 12:15 A.M.)

Water and the clouds have one thing in common: beauty in their radiance. As I see the sun reflecting its magic on the water, I can't help feeling pulled into its trance.

I am embracing and kissing the sun. As the wind blows gently in rhythm with the waves, I can't help raising my arms in the air, and be lifted by the aroma of its spell.

I am being kissed by the waves.

I am kissing the sun and the waves as they gently yet forcefully kiss the sand, the shores, endlessly in present time.

BE STILL

(12:39 A.M.)

Wind, water, and waves rock me to the core of my soul. My Maker, My Creator moves with purpose with its flow.

I am speechless as He calls for me to sit awhile and listen closely at His echoing peaceful call.

Be still! Exhale! Renew!

No troubles, be still... exhale, renew, peacefully, and gently He calls.